Satsuki

Satsuki

Alexander Kennedy

Splatt Press

First published in Great Britain in 1995 by
Alexander Kennedy,
Splatt Pottery, Tresmeer,
 Launceston, Cornwall PL15 8QX

ISBN 0 9525145 0 8

Printed in Great Britain by the Troutbeck Press,
Antron Hill, Mabe, Penryn, Cornwall.

Contents

Dedication

With thanks to my wife Wai Yuk.

Thanks are also due to Peter Mitchell for all his help on this project; to Ray and Geoff of Plymouth Bonsai Society; and to all those people who started out as customers and became good friends - especially Brian Johnson, whose enthusiasm helps keep me inspired.

NOTE: All specialised Japanese terms used in this book are printed in *bold italics.* Explanations of these terms can be found in the Glossary at the end of the book.

Introduction

Satsuki have been described as Japan's most precious floral offering to the West. Those who have the chance to see Satsuki at their best will probably be inclined to agree. Yet in Britain at least, even confirmed Azalea enthusiasts seem to have little idea of what Satsuki are.

Perhaps the principal reason for this slow appreciation of Satsuki by Western azalea growers, is the extreme difference in the cultivation techniques used for these plants, when compared to the familiar "Japanese" garden azalea.

The evergreen garden azalea is seen as an appropriate plant for a wild or woodland garden. Care for such azaleas is very simple and often consists of little more than an occasional application of mulch. The type of care accorded to the typical Satsuki in Japan is a great contrast to this. They tend to be grown as pampered show plants, grown in containers and subject to extensive grooming and trimming.

This book discusses Satsuki mainly from the point of view of bonsai training. It is important to realise, however, that most Satsuki grown in Japan are not considered to be bonsai, they are grown primarily in order to enjoy their breath-taking flowers. The care and training techniques applied to such plants are broadly the same as those used for Satsuki bonsai, but the ultimate aim in this case is to maximise the floral display, rather than to create a powerful image of a tree. This side of the Satsuki hobby is still undiscovered in Britain, because so far it is only the bonsai enthusiasts who tend to be aware of Satsuki at all.

Section One
Background

Chapter One

Origins
and
History

Satsuki and Tsutsuji

The Kinshi Makura

Azaleas enjoyed their first great wave of popularity in Japan during the 17th century. In 1692, a Tokyo nursery-man named **Ito Ihei** wrote the world's first monograph on the subject of azaleas.

This book, the "***Kinshi Makura***" (A Brocade Pillow) was published in five volumes, from hand-cut woodblocks. **Ito** wrote the book in an attempt to bring a sense of order to the hundreds of new azalea varieties which had flooded the market during the preceding decades. Central to **Ito's** system of description was the division of azaleas into two groups:- *Tsutsuji* and Satsuki.

The term *Tsutsuji* covered the many spring-flowering, evergreen azalea species and their hybrids. Plants from this group were the forerunners of the evergreen garden azaleas we know in the West today. Interestingly, when Japanese use the English word "azalea", it is always meant as a translation of the term *Tsutsuji*, rather than in the wider sense that would seem natural in the West.

While *Tsutsuji* were plants which provided brilliant colour in the garden, Satsuki were the aristocrats of the azalea world, used primarily as container-grown show plants.

Mie Satsuki

Mie Satsuki (also referred to as hedge Satsuki) are used for planting out in Japanese gardens. This particular type is quite distinct from the bulk of Satsuki varieties used for container culture. They are used to form the clipped mounds which are a great feature of traditional Japanese garden design. Flowers are of minor importance in the case of *Mie* Satsuki; the main characteristics they are chosen for are response to frequent pruning and an attractive bronze winter foliage. These plants do flower, but in most cases the blooms are still the plain pink of their wild forebears.

The Name Satsuki

The word Satsuki consists of two Japanese *kanji* characters; "*Sa*", which is an old term for five, and "*Tsuki*", which is the word for moon. Satsuki therefore means fifth moon, in other words the fifth month of the oriental lunar calendar. This is equivalent to around June in our calendar and refers to the flowering period, as Satsuki flower around late May or early June.

Wild Parentage

Satsuki are primarily derived from just two species, Rhododendron indicum, the "river satsuki", and Rhododendron tamurae (syn. eriocarpum), known as the "round-leaved satsuki". Some modern botanists have suggested that other species must have been involved because crossing wild plants of these two species does not give rise to all Satsuki characteristics. Other experts oppose this view, pointing out that plants found today in the wild do not reflect the original, very diverse plant population, because all unusual and interesting wild specimens have long since been collected by either professional plant hunters or amateur gardeners.

During the twentieth century, other types of azalea have, on occasion, been used in the production of new Satsuki hybrids. The Belgian Indian Hybrid azalea, "Mme. Moreux" is widely documented as a parent of several successful varieties.

The Continuing Popularity of Satsuki

From the very start, Satsuki were show plants and were frequently grown in containers. At first the potted Satsuki were not trained as bonsai but were merely clipped to maintain size and shape. Any training would have been limited to maximising the display of flowers. Many of these potted Satsuki would have been displayed at annual "Satsuki festivals" which are still held in Japan today.

Enthusiasm for Satsuki has continued ever since the 17th century, with cycles of rising and waning popularity. Throughout the late nineteenth and twentieth centuries there has been a series of great Satsuki booms. Each fresh wave of popularity was the result of new varieties or types catching the imagination of the Japanese public. One of the great enthusiasms of the nineteenth century was the development of Satsuki with variegated leaves. In the nineteen-twenties and -thirties it was very large showy blooms that caught the imagination of the Satsuki growers. Some varieties with huge flowers, as much as five inches across, were produced at this time and these led to an impression among many western azalea growers that the distinguishing feature of Satsuki was large flower size.

By contrast, the most recent Satsuki boom, in the nineteen sixties, featured varieties with small flowers. This was partly because Satsuki growers were by then interested in training their plants as highly sophisticated bonsai and therefore small flowers were felt to be more appropriate. Another factor, however, was that interesting and elegant flower form had become just as important as size or colour, and that many of the most elegant and beautifully shaped flowers were of smaller size.

This last great boom peaked in the early nineteen seventies, when growers in Japan were propagating over thirty million Satsuki cuttings per year. Inevitably, the market became flooded and prices collapsed. The production methods used by the big producers, involving the use of heated greenhouses to promote rapid growth, had in any case become uneconomic in the face of rising energy prices. Many thousands of young Satsuki plants were planted out to grow on at this time. These plants grew into many of the fine Satsuki bonsai being trained and exhibited in Japan today.

Satsuki with variegated foliage were once very popular. This variety is **Shira-fuji,** *which has white and purple flowers.*

*ABOVE: The classic **saizaki** variety, **Kinsai,** is excellent for bonsai training.*

Chapter Two

Satsuki
as
Bonsai

Satsuki Characteristics

Although Satsuki have always been grown primarily for their flowers, they have many other characteristics which make them highly desirable for bonsai training.

Leaves

Leaves vary in size from variety to variety but all can be described as small or very small. As a bonsai they therefore tend to have foliage with a very good sense of scale. Although evergreen, Satsuki drop a set of old leaves in autumn. These generally first turn an attractive shade of red or yellow, giving a beautiful two-tone effect with the dark green younger leaves. The foliage of some varieties will also change to an attractive bronze colour during the winter period, further increasing the seasonal variations.

Trunk

For many enthusiasts it is the wonderful, massive trunks displayed by old Satsuki which make them so special as bonsai. Even at a young age, Satsuki naturally develop a strongly buttressed surface root system. As well as superb rootage, it is possible to produce trunks with tremendous taper and character.

Satsuki bark has a special attractiveness of its own. Though the bark of natural trunks is usually dark brown and slightly flaky, when it is regularly brushed and washed it is smooth and varies from mottled bronze to pale grey or tan.

Response to pruning

A major attraction of Satsuki for bonsai training is their ability to produce new shoots anywhere on the trunk or branches, even from very old wood. This, coupled with the capacity to develop branch and twig structures rapidly, makes it possible to produce new branches exactly where the design of a bonsai dictates. Since they are so amenable to selective pruning and detail wiring, a branch on a Satsuki can easily be trained to exactly the form and profile desired.

Flowers

Early bonsai books in English suggested that the large size of Satsuki flowers made them rather unsuitable subjects for high class bonsai. This assertion misses the point entirely. As with almost every other flowering bonsai, the illusion of "tree-ness" is difficult, or impossible, to sustain when in flower. The point is, Satsuki offer the prospect of having bonsai of the very highest quality for 11 months of the year. These bonsai are then transformed, for a few weeks in May or June, into one of the finest potted flowering plants in existence.

Bonsai styling

If left to grow naturally, a Satsuki will form a sprawling, rounded bush. As with many other shrub-type plants used for bonsai, it does not have a natural tree form of its own. The styles used in training Satsuki bonsai are therefore borrowed from images of other trees.

Japanese will tell you that Satsuki are usually grown in a "Pine tree" style, or manner. This does not mean that they resemble pine trees found in nature, however; merely that the basic formal rules underlying the styling are those considered applicable to bonsai pines. These same styling rules-of-thumb are very commonly used in Japan whenever a Bonsai subject does not have a definable style of its own.

NOTE: *This use of the word* **style** *must not be confused with the more common use of the term, where it refers to contrasting bonsai designs (Informal upright, Cascade, etc.). A bonsai can be a Literati, Windswept or an Informal upright, for instance, and still be what the Japanese term - "styled in a pine tree manner".*

To experienced western bonsai practitioners, a large percentage of Satsuki exhibited in Japan do not seem particularly well styled. Though the Satsuki in Japanese shows may have trunks much superior to any in the West, the foliage on many of them appears much too dense. (This characteristic, where individual branch lines are lost and the foliage becomes one shrub-like mass, is also a criticism levelled at many lesser quality Japanese pine bonsai.)

Although peak flowering performance requires fairly free growth in the preceding year, this still does not explain the heaviness of so many otherwise very fine Japanese Satsuki bonsai. Perhaps it is simply a matter of prevailing taste, or perhaps there is a wish to capture some of the feeling of the clipped mound effect which is the enduring image of azaleas in Japanese gardens. The important point to note is that Satsuki bonsai do not have to have this dense, heavy appearance; it is a matter of choice on the part of the grower.

NOTE: *The following section discusses Bonsai styles as they apply to Satsuki particularly. If the readers wish to learn more about bonsai styling in general, they should consult one of the many excellent introductory books on bonsai. A number of these are mentioned under Further Reading, at the back of this book.*

The bonsai styles used for Satsuki

Satsuki have the potential to be developed in most of the commonly used bonsai styles. Unfortunately, since most growers are forced to resort to a commercially grown plant if they want a bonsai of any substance, their options tend to be narrowed down to either the Repeated "S" style, or the Informal upright.

Repeated "S" style

This form evolved when Satsuki were still considered to be more "potted flowering plants", rather than bonsai. The aim was to produce a tall plant with a large volume of foliage and thus a stunning display of flowers. The bends in the trunk enabled large foliage pads to be developed which were offset from those above, thus allowing even light to all parts of the plant.

In Japanese Satsuki exhibitions, Repeated "S" trees are entered for classes where the plants are judged solely on their flowering performance. Such plants are often referred to as "*Meika*". Growers who compete in these *Meika* classes are often quite distinct from those exhibiting Satsuki bonsai at the same shows.

Repeated "S" style

Meika trees are grown with lots of branches, so that in flower they form a large, unbroken mass of colour. Much space in current Japanese Satsuki magazines is devoted to instruction on converting *Meika* type Repeated "S" trunks into more sophisticated bonsai designs. If a trunk has bends which are not too extreme or unnatural, the lower branches can be removed and the much reduced upper branches restyled to form a Literati design.

Informal Upright style

This term really covers a very wide range of different designs. Informal upright Satsuki currently being grown and shown in Japan can be split into a number of distinct categories.

"Fuji" Informal style

1) A fattened Repeated "S" style. This type of curvaceous Informal Upright is not very naturalistic but can be most attractive. Most of the best Satsuki imported into Europe would probably fall into this category.

2) The "Mount Fuji" style. Some Japanese growers devote their efforts to producing bonsai with short trunks that have very extreme taper, so that the trunk bears some resemblance to a miniature Mount Fuji. Such trees are commonly developed with a very simple cap of dense foliage.

3) The classic Informal Upright style. The most sophis-

ticated growers of Satsuki bonsai in Japan, are now developing trees with much more naturalistic forms. Satsuki trunks which have very distinctive curves, fissures, etc., yet still achieve a very natural look are desirable indeed and fetch extremely high prices.

Other styles

A grower developing Satsuki from young material will find that almost all of the traditional bonsai styles can be used or adapted for this species. Even unlikely choices such as a classic Broom style are possible. The Literati form is one that is often employed for tall, slender Satsuki, but this is one of the least successful designs for this plant. This is because the smooth bark is somehow unable to supply sufficient ruggedness to the image.

Cascade style

Styles which are particularly worthy of consideration include Cascade, Root-over-rock and Raft or Clump forms.

Given its basal dominance, the Satsuki is admirably suited to training as a Cascade. This is a style which offers immense freedom for abstract composition, and which, when covered in flowers, can give an impression of a stunning waterfall of colour.

Many Japanese Satsuki are grown in the Root-over-rock style. Major roots on a Satsuki will swell and knit together quite quickly, forming an interesting, gnarled, but smooth-barked mass, so it is an ideal species for this technique. For the same reasons, Satsuki are also very popular for training in the *Neagari*, or Exposed-Root style. The Neagari style does not come across well in reproduction, but some large examples in Japan are very powerful images when seen in the flesh. This seems very much a style to tackle on a large scale, however, small Exposed-Root bonsai rarely seem to escape from looking weedy.

Satsuki offer great potential for developing multiple-trunk bonsai. They can be grown as groups, though these are rarely seen. Raft or Clump style trees offer multiple trunks, together with the chance to produce a massive spread of surface rootage, which can be one of Satsuki's most impressive features. The normal problems of complexity found in most multiple-trunk bonsai can be magnified by the Satsuki's very dense and rapidly growing foliage. The secrets of managing these complex designs are to establish simplified rhythms through the design and to scrupulously maintain the negative spaces between foliage masses.

Clump style

Chapter Three

Flower Colours and Types

Satsuki Flowers

Few plant groups have flowers which vary so much in form, size, colour and markings as do Satsuki. Add to this the possibility of a number of flower types occurring together on one plant and it is easy to see how these flowers can become the focus of a passionate enthusiasm.

Flower Size

Flower size varies enormously from variety to variety. Japanese publications often class Satsuki blooms in five or more size ranges, but small, medium and large classifications are probably adequate. A size of between 4cm and 5cm would be considered small, while medium-sized flowers would fall into the 5cm to 7cm band. A large Satsuki flower can be anything from 7cm up to 12cm or even more.

The preferred flower size has changed over time with peaks of popularity for both large and small types. In the period between the two world wars, Japanese Satsuki breeders strove to produce varieties with ever bigger blooms. Large-flowered varieties such as *Shuku-fuku*, *Tama-no-hada* and *Hi-gasa* are very spectacular. If grown as bonsai however, such varieties really need to be developed as large trees. Enormous, four- or five-inch blooms can look rather grotesque on a bonsai of modest proportions.

Since the nineteen-sixties, small-flowered varieties have been very much the most popular. Today it is felt that these smaller flowers are more in keeping with the sense of scale implied by bonsai training. (The smallness of the flowers is of course only a matter of degree; it is hard to argue that any Satsuki actually looks like a tree while it is in flower.) Above all, fashion in the period since the sixties has favoured the

Flower Size

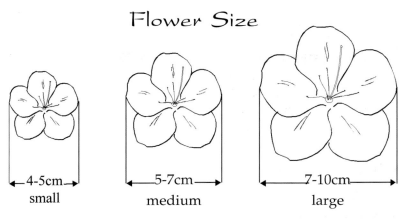

4-5cm	5-7cm	7-10cm
small	medium	large

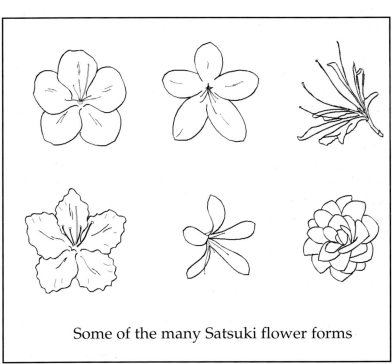

Some of the many Satsuki flower forms

Kozan family, with its many interesting branch sports.

Flower Forms

It is unlikely that any other single group of plants shows such a huge variation in flower form as do Satsuki. Flowers are generally single, but both semi-double and double types exist, as well as hose-in-hose types. The flower typically has five petals, though sometimes there are six or more. Petals can be rounded and overlapping; or they can be pointed and separate, giving a star-like effect. In some cases (known as *saizaki*) the petals are long thin and distorted, e.g. *Kinsai*; or they can be almost totally absent, e.g. *Shiraito-no-taki*. Petals can also range from flat and smooth to wavy with frilly edges, as well as varying in texture between very firm and soft.

Flower Patterns

The range of beautiful colour markings found on Satsuki blooms is vast. In addition to solid-coloured flowers (selfs), which may themselves have a throat blotch in a darker or contrasting colour, Japanese sources distinguish and name over twenty different multi-colour patterns. To western eyes, some of these patterns look remarkably similar, but learning to spot and distinguish the many subtle variations is one of the joys of these beautiful plants.

Most of the colour patterns are described as types of "*shibori*" (variegation, or literally "tie-dye pattern"). Any but the most dedicated enthusiast is likely to find learning the Japanese pattern names rather demanding. Two terms that are very useful for discussing Satsuki flowers, however, are *sokojiro* (white throat) and *fukurin* (jewel border).

Sokojiro

Fukurin

Hanzome

Date-shibori

Hakeme-shibori

Arare-shibori

Harusame

Tobiiri-shibori

*Single colour
(with blotch)*

Tamafu

Another pattern, unique to Satsuki, which deserves to be remembered by name is *tamafu* (white jewel spot). This describes the distinctive pale smudge of colour down the centre of each petal, found on such varieties as **Yata-no-kagami** and **Shin-kyo**.

Flower Colour

The wild Rhododendron indicum generally has reddish-pink flowers, with occasional plants bearing white blooms. The other main Satsuki parent, Rhododendron tamurae, has mostly red or purplish flowers with some white or pink variations.

In modern Satsuki, the colour range extends from orange, through pink and red, to crimson and purple, as well as white. There are no yellows or blues to be found among the evergreen azaleas. Also missing are any really dark-coloured blooms. Even with these limitations, the available colour choice is very rich. The colour variety is made even richer by the fact that combinations of colour on one plant are so common.

Chapter Four

Propagating True to Type

The Problem of Sports

A common question asked when people first see Satsuki in flower is "why have we never seen or heard of these plants before?".

Factors contributing to their slow acceptance in the West have included doubtful winter hardiness, and the fact that they are at their best when grown in containers and given regular pruning. Another major problem, however, is the difficulty of adequately describing particular varieties and ensuring propagation true to type.

The tendency to produce branch sports is one of the great attractions of Satsuki. This means that different parts of the same plant can have totally different flowers. Indeed, several distinct flower patterns can often occur together on one mature Satsuki plant.

Our conventional western idea of a variety would include a definitive description of the flower's appearance, but this is obviously inadequate for Satsuki. A Japanese description of a Satsuki variety includes all the flower patterns and colours which a mature plant of that type will (eventually) produce. This is a much looser use of the term "variety" than we are used to, especially as plants may take many years to show the full range of potential flower patterns, even if they are true to type.

The concept of a Satsuki variety becomes even more tenuous when it is realised that not all cuttings from a given plant will grow to bear all the flower types of that same variety. In fact, what the Japanese refer to as a "variety" is perhaps better thought of as a "selected strain". Whether a cutting can be called true to type is assessed on the basis of its actual appearance, not simply on its parentage.

34

*The variety **Dai-seiko** has mainly white flowers with occasional pink variants. This particular plant bears only pink blossoms but is still very attractive.*

35

*The variety **Hiodoshi** is an excellent variety of the **sokojiro** type.*

An attractive Satsuki on display in an exhibition.

This large import will make a very fine specimen in a few years; once the branch structure has been developed. The same tree is shown in flower on page 95.

Western horticulture, or at least the modern commercial nurseryman, is not able to work with plants described in such loose terms. Our "Garden Centre" culture leads us to expect a colour photograph with every plant and that this will be an accurate depiction of what we are buying.

Western horticulturists have always seen sporting behaviour in plants as a flaw which should be rooted out. The Japanese, on the other hand, have always seen plants which sport different flowers as special treasures, to be valued for these characteristics regardless of any problems they cause with propagation and description. Not only with azaleas but also with plants such as camellias and flowering apricots, favoured varieties in Japan often sport different coloured flowers. Such plants would probably have been ruthlessly eliminated by western nurserymen.

Selection of Cutting Material

Though cuttings taken at random do not necessarily produce plants with the same range of flowers as the parent plant, it is possible to select shoots which give the required characteristics with a fair degree of certainty. The best Japanese nurserymen take a great deal of trouble to record which branches should be used for cuttings. For western nurserymen, such meticulous recording procedures would present great difficulties, as they have no experience with such systems.

Selection of branches in order to obtain flowers which resemble those on the stock plant varies with the variety. A very typical Satsuki variety which features *shibori* (tie-dyed)

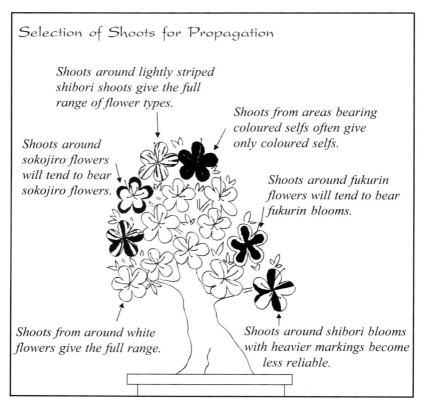

Selection of Shoots for Propagation

Shoots around lightly striped shibori shoots give the full range of flower types.

Shoots from areas bearing coloured selfs often give only coloured selfs.

Shoots around sokojiro flowers will tend to bear sokojiro flowers.

Shoots around fukurin flowers will tend to bear fukurin blooms.

Shoots from around white flowers give the full range.

Shoots around shibori blooms with heavier markings become less reliable.

type flowers, will also carry pure white self-coloured blooms and selfs of the contrast colour (usually pink or red). Often there will be both a darker and a lighter form of the contrast colour self. Many varieties will also bear *sokojiro* or *fukurin* type blossoms.

When propagating from such a plant the likely outcomes are as follows:-

1) Branches bearing *shibori* flowers which are mostly white will generally yield the full colour range of the parent plant. *Shibori* flowers which are heavily marked with the

contrast colour are much less reliable.

2) Branches with white self flowers will usually yield plants of the parent type, though in certain varieties they give rise to pure white offspring.

3) Branches bearing selfs in the paler form of the contrast colour tend to give cuttings which show both paler and darker coloured selfs. (In the USA, nurserymen often refer to such plants as the #2 form of the variety.)

4) Shoots from branches bearing dark-coloured selfs will commonly give plants with only dark self-coloured flowers. (Sometimes termed the #3 form of the plant.)

5) Shoots from branches with *sokojiro* or *fukurin* type flowers will generally produce flowers only of that pattern.

Mixed-up Genes

New cells in a plant are formed by cell-division in a special area called the cambium layer. Each cell in the cambium layer carries a complete set of genetic instructions for growing a new plant; it is this which makes propagation by cuttings, etc., possible. Through mutation, the genetic information in some cambium cells can be changed, and all new cells formed when these divide will also carry the changes. A new branch grows from an adventitious bud, which is formed by the division of a cluster of cells in the cambium layer. If the cells are all of the new, mutated type, then the branch will be purely of this new type. If the cluster of cells includes both old and new types, then the new branch will also carry cells of both forms.

If you are uncertain as to which branches should be used for cutting material, one fairly safe rule would be to choose those that seem to have the most typical flowers. e.g. on a *saizaki* variety, take cuttings only from areas with *saizaki* flowers. Branches reverting to full-petalled flowers are likely to yield plants with these full-petalled flowers only.

None of the above rules of thumb offer a guarantee that propagations will flower true to type. Fresh mutations within the plant material can occur, which can lead to different flower types; but the major problem is that each branch already carries a complex mixture of varied genetic material. The information which determines flower colour is carried within the cambium layer of the plant. Thus the colour of flowers on any new shoot is determined by the cambium material from which that shoot arises on the parent branch. In a variety with complex flower patterns, there will be different "types" of cambium around the circumference of the branches. On a branch with striped flowers, the stripes actually indicate which parts of the shoot's circumference carry which colour.

Striping on a flower can indicate the colours carried by adjacent shoots

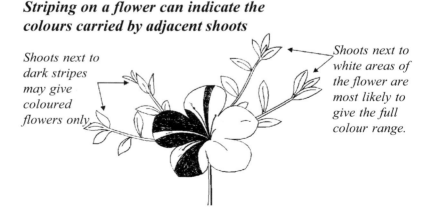

Shoots next to dark stripes may give coloured flowers only

Shoots next to white areas of the flower are most likely to give the full colour range.

It is important to keep a sense of proportion about these propagation problems.. Young plants from an attractive Satsuki will themselves bear attractive flowers, even if they are not in the full colour range of the parent. In the case of some varieties, plants which bear only one part of the colour range may be very desirable, or even preferred; for example *Eikan#2*, a pink self form of the variety *Eikan* is much prized for bonsai work.

New varieties

Although many new varieties have come from seedlings, most new plants named today are aberrant branch sports of existing varieties. When a Satsuki produces flowers with a new form or with different colour combinations, efforts are made to propagate from this atypical material. The resulting plants are then given a new variety name. The popular variety *Kozan* has given rise to many new varieties in this manner.

Varietal Drift

Given the unstable, sporting nature of Satsuki plants and the problems in propagation, it is almost inevitable that the type plant of a variety will change somewhat over time. That the Japanese growers have managed to keep the distinctive features of many varieties quite fixed over hundreds of years is a great testimony to their self-discipline. By contrast, it is noticeable that plants propagated from stock imported into the USA only a few decades ago, already seem to have descriptions which differ substantially from the Japanese type.

A system for indentifying Satsuki branches

Knowing which flower types are borne by particular branches on a Satsuki plant is not only important when cuttings are to be taken; it can also be essential to have this information when pruning. For instance, if a bonsai bears mainly white flowers with only one or two small branches showing an attractive contrasting colour, it could be very important not to cut these particular branches off.

It is difficult, or impossible, to remember these flowering patterns; there is also no practical way of recording the information on paper (though photographs are always a help). The solution is to mark the plant itself while it is in flower. In Japan the common practice is to mark important branches, such as those to be used for cuttings, by fixing a piece of wire loosely around them. It is possible to develop this into a more sophisticated system, by using coloured plastic bag ties (as used in the kitchen). Different branches can be marked with different coloured ties to represent different things. Such a system would, in addition, require the maintenance of written records to provide a key to the colour codes.

Chapter Five

Cultural Requirements

Basic Satsuki Needs

Soil

Satsuki are "lime-hating" ericaceous plants which require an acid soil to thrive. A pH range from 4.5 to just over 6.0 is tolerated. Providing that lime levels are low, however, there is no need for the soil to be strongly acid. A pH of 6.0 will be found quite adequate. If the soil mix satisfies this requirement, then there is a lot of flexibility regarding the actual ingredients used.

The important physical characteristics of the potting medium are that it should be sufficiently porous and that it should drain freely while still retaining a moderately high level of moisture. Adequate pore space is very important because, although Satsuki roots require constant even dampness, they also require the presence of air in order to function. Azaleas rapidly succumb to root rot in waterlogged soils.

In the West, azalea potting mixtures have traditionally been based on peat: in Japan, the acid sub-soil known as *Kanuma-tsuchi* forms the principal potting ingredient.

Kanuma has a poor reputation with some British bonsai enthusiasts. This is generally because their experience of the material has been limited to working with imported trees which are several years overdue for re-potting. In that situation, the Satsuki roots grow through every *Kanuma* particle, binding them together into something resembling a "cream-coloured concrete block". Re-potting a tree in this state can be a very frustrating and time-consuming experience. If bonsai are re-potted in good time, however, *Kanuma* is a very pleasant material to use. If available, it is an excellent choice for potting finished bonsai, despite its high cost.

While *Kanuma* can be used on its own for bonsai, in Japan it is mixed with anything up to 50% of chopped sphagnum moss. The higher percentages of moss are used following severe root disturbance. In addition to supplying additional moisture retention, sphagnum also seems to play a part in promoting fresh root growth.

Other soil mixes quoted by Japanese sources include various mixtures of *Kanuma*, peat, grit and *Akadama*; e.g. 50% *Kanuma* and the remaining 50% split evenly among the other ingredients.

A good starting point for a potting compost using western ingredients would be 50% long-fibred coarse peat (or a good peat substitute), 30% pumice or calcined clay (e.g. "Biosorb") and 20% grit. If available, up to 50% percent *Kanuma* could be added to this mix.

For young pre-bonsai plants putting on vigorous growth, a mix containing more humus will work well; e.g. 75% long-fibred peat (or good peat substitute) and 25% pumice. *Kanuma* does not seem especially suitable for young plants being rapidly grown on. I have found that young cuttings consistently put on more growth in a peat-based mix than in *Kanuma*.

Water

Given the "lime-hating" character of azaleas, they are much easier to maintain if a supply of soft, acid water is readily available. In areas with hard tap water, growers may have to consider a means of collecting rain water. Where there is no alternative to using tap water in such areas, various things can be done to ease the situation. One option would be to use a much more acid soil medium, as this would be better able to neutralise the effect of the added lime. Use of a small amount of soil acidifier added to the water will also prove helpful. One easily obtainable acidifier is "Miracid", though the fact that this is also a fertilizer might cause difficulties during the winter dormant period. Another acidifier recommended by growers in hard water areas is phosphoric acid. If you can obtain phosphoric acid diluted to 10% with water, then an occasional addition of this (one teaspoon per gallon of water) will re-establish the required acidity levels.

Fertilizer

Azaleas are basically poor-soil plants. Therefore, their nutrient requirements are moderately low. This does not mean that rapid growth cannot be promoted by heavier feeding, but growers should be aware that overfeeding problems can arise, particularly when plants are grown in small containers.

Some sources report that Satsuki are choosy about their fertilizers. I have found no evidence of this, but it would be prudent either to stick to fertilizers recommended for azaleas, or to test any new feed before putting it to general use.

Suitable ericaceous fertilizers include granular feeds such as "Enmag" and the excellent liquid feed and soil-acidifier "Miracid". Japanese growers use organic feeds for their Satsuki bonsai and an imported organic such as "Biogold" gives superb results.

Feed should be given throughout the growing season, except for a period from early May until after flowering.

Some growers consider a feed of 0-10-10 fertilizer is desirable in late summer. This is said to be helpful for flower bud development, but I have never found it essential. Azalea roots remain slightly active throughout the winter and feeding should be continued quite late into the autumn. A final feed should be given when the spring leaves change colour.

Satsuki require chelated trace elements as part of their feeding programme. If these are not included in the fertilizers used, they should be supplied separately in the form of a spring feed of "Sequestrene" or similar product.

Satsuki pests

Azaleas are relatively free of insect pest problems. Although a number of exotic azalea-specific pests are listed in Galle's monograph, the most common foliage infestations in the U.K. are likely to be aphids and the odd caterpillar. These are easily dealt with using proprietary insecticides.

Red Spider Mite is occasionally mentioned as a problem, but this is generally a pest which thrives in dry greenhouse conditions, rather than the more humid air preferred by Satsuki. Red spider mite can be both difficult to detect and difficult to eliminate. Proprietary chemicals recommended for this pest should be used, but repeated treatments may be necessary to eradicate an infestation.

Vine Weevil is currently the insect pest most feared by growers of Satsuki (and all other bonsai). The adults do not generally cause severe damage, though they do chew Satsuki foliage. It is the soil-borne vine weevil grub which causes potentially fatal damage to plant roots. These grubs can destroy the root system - of young plants in particular - before the grower is even aware there is a problem. Female vine weevils are able to reproduce parthenogenetically, so large populations can build up extremely quickly. It has been stated that one female vine weevil is capable of laying 10,000 eggs.

The vine weevil is extremely resistant to most insecticides. Gamma BHC powder mixed into the compost gives a good measure of control, however. Another option is to treat all the plants in a collection with parasitic nematodes which destroy the grubs. Other, more effective, chemical treatments are now becoming available to the horticultural trade, but are not on sale to the general public due to their high toxicity.

Yet another option for vine weevil control relies on the fact that the adults cannot fly. If Satsuki are kept isolated from the ground on raised benches, it is possible to apply bands of grease around all the legs of these benches, on which the adults can be trapped and killed. With a little thought, all new purchases could be given a separate, grease-protected quarantine bench to keep any emerging weevils isolated.

Fungal diseases

Root-rot

The most serious disease problem encountered by Satsuki growers is fungal root rot caused by various Phytophthora organisms. The first symptoms to be observed are usually the wilting and dropping of a plants leaves, but the damage has actually occurred at the fine feeder roots. If the roots are examined they will appear brown rather than a healthy white colour.

Basic hygiene measures should be maintained at all times in order to prevent a build-up of infection, but these organisms are extremely widespread, attacking thousands of different plant types and able to survive for very long periods without a host.

High soil moisture levels are the principal factor in triggering an attack of root rot, as the fungal spores require a film of free water in order to move through the soil. Use of a well-drained compost and careful control of water are thus major factors in the prevention of this disease. The other key procedure is a regular preventative spraying regime, using a suitable systemic fungicide.

Foliage diseases

The other regularly encountered fungal problems are likely to be powdery-mildew-type infections of the foliage, and azalea gall.

Mildews are almost always a symptom of poor ventilation. In general, they are only encountered when Satsuki are crowded together in winter quarters where they are surrounded by still, damp air. Mildews are easily controlled by systemic sprays and an improvement in environmental conditions.

Azalea gall is a disfiguring disease where leaves, or other parts of the plant, swell into large hard lumps. Fortunately, this disease is rarely a serious threat to the plant's health. The fungus is spread only externally, not through the plant tissues. Removal and disposal of galls, preferably by burning, before they reach the infective, powdery stage can prevent its spread. Certain Satsuki varieties seem much more prone than others to this problem and its incidence varies greatly from year to year. Humid, shady conditions are a factor in encouraging the disease, and a move to a more open airy position is often all that is required to effect a cure. Fungicidal sprays are also fairly effective, particularly the traditional copper-based sprays..

Winter Protection

Satsuki azaleas are quite hardy when grown in the open ground on the South coast of England. In areas which are subject to hard frosts, however, they may be subject to damage in severe weather if they are not given protection. This applies even more when plants are grown in containers.

In general, the bigger and the more mature a plant is, the better it will stand up to cold weather. Young material, up to two or three years of age, should be regarded as tender. Frost damage on these small plants usually takes the form of the bark splitting away from the wood. Such splits are easily recognised and should be sealed with *Kiyonal*, "Cut-paste", or some similar product. If the damage is not too severe, plants will recover, though growth may remain weak for a considerable period.

Large Satsuki will usually stand several degrees of frost for a short time, but the degree of hardiness seems to vary from variety to variety. My own experience would indicate that slow-growing, dwarf types are often less hardy. The general health and vigour of the individual plant almost certainly play a part as well.

If a Satsuki is a treasured possession, it would be foolish not to give it a little protection in frosty weather. In all but the most severe frosts, a cold greenhouse will provide all the protection required. For young cuttings or weak trees, an additional covering with insulating fleece might also be needed. This material would also be useful as a more general protective covering during unusually prolonged or heavy frosts. The rare British winter which is severe enough to require even better frost protection than this is almost certainly going to damage other bonsai species as well. On such occasions, some form of background heating for the greenhouse could be a life-saver, but this might only be needed once in every seven to ten years in most parts of Britain.

If a grower does not have access to a greenhouse, Satsuki can be protected by placing them in a garage or shed for a day or two during a cold snap. If protection is needed for longer periods, then adequate light must be supplied. Another option would be to bring the Satsuki into a cool room within the house (e.g. an unheated porch).

The above paragraphs refer to British conditions. Satsuki enthusiasts in other parts of the world keep plants in climates with much more severe winters. In such circumstances, the grower has to devise much more efficient frost protection for overwintering.

Satsuki as indoor plants

Though Satsuki are considered hardy or near-hardy, they adapt relatively well to indoor culture. When provided with suitable temperatures and light levels during the winter months, they will continue to grow for twelve months of the year without any apparent ill-effects. The most rapid way to develop a young Satsuki plant is to grow it in a heated greenhouse. (This method was used for commercial Satsuki production in Japan before rising fuel prices rendered it uneconomic.)

All of the above would suggest that Satsuki would

make much better indoor trees than many of the sub-tropical Chinese species which are sold under the description of "Indoor bonsai". The problem would be that Satsuki kept in indoor conditions would be unlikely to flower reliably, if at all, unless the grower could provide a means of cold-setting the flower buds.

A Satsuki bonsai illustrating the appearance of branch profiles after a major pruning and rewiring.

A specimen Satsuki with a massive trunk base.

This small bonsai of the variety Kozan is an example of a very good imported tree. Although the branches will require a few years of development, the trunk is excellent with good taper and character.

Very tall Satsuki are sometimes suited to air-layering techniques; thereby creating two new bonsai.

58

Section Two

Training

Chapter Six

Basic Training Principles

The Satsuki Growth Cycle

Unlike the evergreen garden azaleas, Satsuki put on considerable new growth before flowering. A second flush of growth occurs after flowering is finished.

In spring, new shoots commence their growth from beneath the flower buds. From two to five shoots typically grow from each terminal.

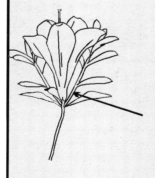

By the time the Satsuki flowers in May or June, the new season's shoots can be from 2" to 6" long. Strong spring growth can "submerge" the flowers, spoiling the display unless it is trimmed.

Flower buds for the following year are formed in mid-summer, so plants should not be pruned after about mid-July.

Although the flower buds are well established and easily visible by the end of the summer, they will not develop fully until they are subject to a period of winter cool.

Immediately after flowering, the shoots begin another period of strong growth. This is an ideal time for pruning and repotting because the plant is in a vigorous state and recovers quickly.

From mid-summer onwards, the next season's flower buds form at the terminals of the current year's growth.

In autumn, the spring leaves change colour and fall.

Pruning Satsuki

The factor which makes Satsuki supreme among flowering bonsai subjects is their wonderful response to pruning.

Satsuki have been grown for over 300 years as potted show-plants and are ideally suited to pruning and shaping. Their close relatives, the *Mie* Satsuki, are grown in Japanese gardens precisely for their ability to respond to sculptural shearing. Japanese people have come to use "Satsuki love to be pruned" as a common saying, in recognition of this central feature of their behaviour.

A great many Japanese enthusiasts are not really interested in bonsai forms as such. Their reason for growing Satsuki lies in the flowers. Their aim in pruning is to develop a branch- and twig-structure which will show off the gorgeous blooms to best effect. The old fashioned "Repeated-"S" style of Satsuki does not attempt to resemble a tree. The structure of these plants is best described as a sort of coat hanger on which the flowers are hung!

Although the aims of those mainly interested in bonsai form may differ from those who pursue floral display, the training techniques employed are generally the same.

Pruning of young growth

When considering the pruning of Satsuki, it is useful to distinguish between two types of new growth. What can be termed mature, or normal, growth shoots are quite compact, typically forming around two to four inches of length in a season. They generally spring from buds at the tips of last year's growth and are distinguished by the fact that

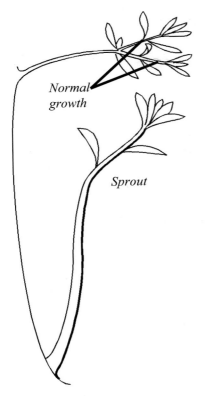

Normal growth

Sprout

they have leaves all along their length.

The other type of new growth is commonly referred to as a "sprout", or shoot. Sprouts are juvenile-type growth which the azalea plant uses to form major new areas of woody structure: additional trunks or major new areas of branches. Sprouts can be distinguished from normal growth by the fact that they are thicker and sturdier. They have leaves only near their tips and, if unchecked, will rapidly elongate to several inches. Although sprouts can appear anywhere on the plant, they commonly spring from older wood. The major sites for sprout growth are at the base of the trunk, branch junctions and around old pruning scars.

Sprouts are not desirable on a finished Satsuki. It is therefore a part of regular maintenance to remove any sprouts as soon as they are spotted.

Sprouts are however, very useful in the development of new Satsuki. They are also the main agent for trunk thickening. Planting in a deep growing-bed and pruning back hard every two years or so, encourages the Satsuki to send out masses of trunk sprouts. The rapid elongation of these sprouts causes rapid thickening of the trunk.

Pruning large branches

In Japan many Satsuki bonsai are created by severe pruning of very large plants, which have been field grown for many years, or decades. This process involves sawing off very substantial branches and replacing them with new growth. Unfortunately, the sudden removal of very large branches can lead to problems. Japanese writers describe the difficulty as "sap withdrawal". When a small branch is pruned, the Satsuki responds by throwing out new buds in the damaged area. When a large branch carrying a significant proportion of the plant's foliage is suddenly removed, however, the area below the cut may die back. Effectively, the Satsuki decides to abandon its growth efforts in the damaged area and concentrate all its energies elsewhere.

Sap Withdrawal

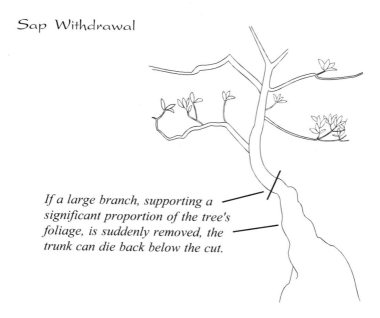

If a large branch, supporting a significant proportion of the tree's foliage, is suddenly removed, the trunk can die back below the cut.

Sap withdrawal is not likely to be a problem with young plants or those which have been growing very vigorously. The size of branch which may give problems is very hard to specify. It might be dangerous to remove a branch of just a quarter-of-an-inch from a weak pot-bound bonsai but a branch well in excess of one-inch in diameter could probably be removed quite safely from a vigorous Satsuki which has just been lifted from a growing bed.

Not all branches are equally prone to sap withdrawal. If the branch removed has live branches left both directly above and below it, then there is no danger, providing that the wound is properly sealed. The main danger branches are at the apex, which is always less vigorous anyway, and bottom branches which do not have other growth for some distance directly above them. In the case of these low branches, the sap paths often die back right down to the ground and the major roots below the branch also die.

When there is a worry of sap withdrawal occurring, the safe approach is to remove the large branch in stages. If all the foliage except for two or three leaves is removed from the branch, and all new buds which subsequently appear on it are rubbed off, then the branch can be removed with safety the following year. This is because the sap flow to that branch will already have slowed down to a trickle. It is also likely that new sprouts will have appeared around the base of the branch. These new sprouts should be left growing because they will help maintain the sap flow when the branch is removed.

An alternative method used by Japanese growers for avoiding sap withdrawal is to saw a wedge out of the branch to about half of its diameter, at the point where it is to be removed. The amount of foliage on the branch is also reduced sharply. The hole left by removing the wedge is filled

with cut-paste to prevent it drying out, and the branch is removed entirely the following spring. Again, the purpose is to cut down the flow of sap in stages rather than all at once.

A wedge extending half-way through the branch is removed and filled with Cut-Paste.

Wiring Satsuki

In Japanese Satsuki nurseries, it is possible to see very large trunks being bent. Yet anyone who tries to shape a Satsuki with wire will soon discover that these plants are very brittle. Some novices rapidly conclude that attempting to bend any branch over about two years old carries an unacceptable degree of risk. Mature Satsuki branches can in fact be shaped very successfully, but the process requires patience, concentration and sound wiring technique.

The first thing to recognize is that breakage points are quite predictable. Snapping is most likely at branch junctions, old pruning scars or other areas where the branch has suffered previous damage. If a breakage does occur on a straight section of branch, it will happen on the outside of the curve, midway between two coils of wire, and at the point of greatest bending stress. A key factor in avoiding breaks is to spot the potential stress points and support them carefully with the fingers as bending is carried out.

Many breaks occur where too heavy a gauge of wire is used for the branch being bent. The stiffness of the wire should always be appropriate to the stiffness of the branch. Carrying the end of a thick wire on along a tapering section of trunk or branch, beyond the point where it is suitable, is a dangerous practice. This is because the hands and fingers can no longer sense the stresses being applied to the branch, due to the effort needed to bend the wire itself. This problem of sensing just how much strain is being applied to a branch can often be eased by applying two strands of thinner wire, rather than one thick one. This makes bending more sensitive and also provides more support. (Contrary to the standard bonsai practice of placing two strands of wire tightly together, some people wiring Satsuki will often space the second wire equidistantly between the coils of the first one. This helps to even out the bending stresses still further.) Where required, a third strand of wire may also be added.

It is possible to achieve a sharp curve more safely by bending the branch to form a more gentle arc at first. The curve is then made progressively sharper in small stages, with about a week or so between bending efforts. Where suitable anchorage points exist, it is possible to use gradually-tightened guy wires to carry out this slow bending process.

If bending a very stiff section of trunk or major branch is crucial to the tree design, the area can be supported with raffia and lengths of wire before bending is attempted.

Another problem with wiring Satsuki is that the bark is very delicate and can be easily scraped away from the wood during bending. This is another situation where wrapping the branch in raffia is of great help. Wrapping the wire with paper is also good practice, and should certainly be considered when wiring fine quality trees.

If bending a branch very carefully does result in cracking, all is not necessarily lost. The crack can be sealed immediately with "Kiyonal" or a similar substance and, provided there is still an intact sap path on the inside of the branch, it should heal successfully. If a branch does snap off entirely, the procedure is to count to ten, then remind yourself that an even-better-shaped replacement can be grown very quickly. It is by no means unknown for owners of tall, leggy Satsuki to commit an indiscretion while shaping the apex, and then to find that their "mistake" has resulted in a shorter, but much superior bonsai.

A problem which does remain when a cracked branch heals is that the area will always remain a very weak spot. Any subsequent attempts to bend the same branch are liable to result in sudden and unexpected breakage.

Aftercare

Aftercare following wiring and pruning processes involves placing the tree in light shade and taking care not to water excessively until the tree has recovered from the shock. (Stressed trees tend to take up less water.) Foliage misting at this time is particularly beneficial.

All wiring should be checked regularly for signs of biting in. This can occur within four to six weeks on a vigorous plant. The first areas to thicken are young (two- or three-year-old) branches which are supporting a lot of vigorous new growth. Thickening is particularly rapid close to where such branches emerge from the trunk or major branch. Regular checks for wire tightening should concentrate on these areas.

Chapter Seven

The
Annual
Care
Cycle

Caring for an Established Bonsai

There is a regular annual sequence of operations involved in maintaining Satsuki. The exact procedures followed depend on the stage of development of the particular plant. This chapter discusses the maintenance of an established bonsai. Treatment of plants in training is discussed in a later chapter.

The Satsuki Year

Tasks involved in maintaining established Satsuki bonsai can be split up according to the point in the growing season. The main tasks for each time of year are listed below. Each point is then discussed in greater detail.

Spring

Light trimming and thinning of new growth as required.

Early May

Stop fertilizing. Select flower buds.

Flowering period (Mid-May / June)

Stop misting foliage. Move Satsuki to a cool, lightly shaded area.

End of flowering period

Remove flower heads. Prune and wire as required. Repot if necessary.

Late Summer and Autumn

Remove any training wire when it shows signs of tightening. Give the plant only the minimal trimming needed to keep it tidy.

Winter

Allow the flower buds the chance to "cold-set". Protect the plants from hard frost.

Care Before Flowering

Once a plant has reached the stage where good flowering performance is required, it is a general rule that trimming should be fairly light in the spring before blooming. There is the ongoing task of removing new growth buds which appear where they are not wanted. Shoots growing downwards beneath the branch profiles and any growing inwards towards the trunk should also be removed.

Thinning and trimming of other new growth is carried out when the new shoots have at least four leaves. Just how hard the shoots should be cut back at this time depends on the variety, the vigour of the particular plant and how it has been trimmed in previous years. There is no great need to be very precise at this time, because shoots which are trimmed back will re-bud very rapidly and will receive more careful selection and trimming after flowering. The intention at this time of year is mainly to maximise the display of flowers. While foliage pads should be kept fairly neat and compact, the main aim is to control shoots which threaten to smother flower bud development.

The wild Rhododendron indicum parent of the Satsuki has strong spring growth, but its relatively large flowers have long flower stalks which lift them clear of the foliage. Many modern Satsuki have small flowers with fairly short flower stalks. If such plants are not trimmed before flowering, the flowers are either buried down within the foliage, or are at least squashed up and left pointing up to the sky. To prevent this, the new shoots on the top of the foliage pad should be trimmed back to two leaves in most cases, though on some vigorous varieties it may be necessary to cut them back right to the base of the current year's growth. Very vigorous trees may need this process carried out two or

more times before flowering, while some of the slower growing dwarf plants will only need the odd shoot cut back at
this time.

Satsuki should be fed in March and April, then fertilizer should be withheld from the beginning of May until
after flowering. This is most important in the case of plants
bearing flowers of *sokojiro* or *tamafu* patterns. Over-feed-
ing in the period before flowering has the effect of turning
blooms of these types into solid-colour selfs. The water
requirements of Satsuki increase dramatically as flowering
approaches. The requirement for constant even dampness
becomes even more crucial at this time. Allowing the soil to
dry out can ruin the developing flower buds.

Foliage misting is generally beneficial for Satsuki but
should be stopped when the flower buds begin their final
burst of growth. Once colour appears in the buds, water
should be supplied to the pot only. Water on the flower
buds or foliage will affect flower quality and shorten the
duration of flowering. The flowers of some varieties mark
very badly if wetted.

Position of trees during flowering

For most of the year, a position in full
sun is ideal for Satsuki. During the
flowering period however, a move to a
cool, shaded area will allow the plant to
give the best possible display. The ideal
spot is out of doors, but covered by some
sort of roof structure. This situation will
keep rain off the flowers and shade the
tree during the hottest part of the day.

Position during flowering

74

Specimen Satsuki on display in a Japanese nursery.

Hundreds of Satsuki awaiting training in a Japanese nursery.

A field-grown trunk awaiting initial styling and potting.

Large Satsuki trunks grown in the Neagari style are very impressive.

Selection of flower buds

As a Satsuki approaches flowering, the flower buds should be thinned out. For established Satsuki it is normal to remove at least one third of the developing buds. Trees which are still in development will progress very much faster if all, or at least the majority, of the flower buds are removed each year. For these young trees in training, the time to do this is as soon as the buds can be broken out without damage to the new shoots beneath them. On mature trees, however, it is much easier to wait until the buds are larger. The buds are very easy to remove just before they show colour.

My own normal practice is to remove up to one third of the buds from the front of the bonsai and two thirds or more from the back, where they are not seen. It is also standard practice to remove rather more buds from the apex, which is the weakest area of the plant. Many growers seem reluctant to carry out this bud thinning, but the result is a much better flowering display. Instead of the flowers being distorted through overcrowding, each flower can open fully. The smaller number of better flowers will still be able to totally cover the foliage.

Thin out the buds to leave only one on each terminal. Buds growing down within the foliage mass should all be removed, as they will not really contribute to the display. (If there are many buds down within the foliage however, it is a sign that the pruning regime has been incorrect during the preceding season.) The general aim in bud selection is to ensure that the flowers will be evenly spaced and clearly visible to the viewer.

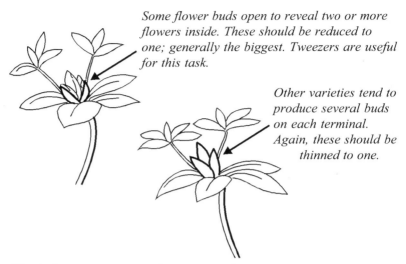

Some flower buds open to reveal two or more flowers inside. These should be reduced to one; generally the biggest. Tweezers are useful for this task.

Other varieties tend to produce several buds on each terminal. Again, these should be thinned to one.

Bud thinning on newly imported trees

Bud thinning can be a very important matter where newly imported trees are concerned. Such trees have been through the stressful process of shipment and will sometimes have been in a fairly weak and pot-bound condition before leaving Japan. Weak and stressed azalea plants will devote even more of their energy to flower production. This gives a massive display of flowers in the year of importation. The end result however, is an even weaker tree which requires a great deal of nursing to return it to full health. Judicious bud thinning of such imported trees can be a great help in reducing stress and will enable a greater proportion of their energy to be devoted to vegetative growth.

Flowering

In this country, the majority of Satsuki will flower sometime between the middle of May and the end of June. The actual flowering dates of a particular plant will vary slightly from year to year depending on the weather and other cultural factors, but different varieties will generally follow each other in the same sequence each year. (Newly imported trees often flower later during the first year than they do in subsequent seasons.)

Growers sometimes need to have their bonsai flowering on a particular date (e.g. for a show). In this situation it is possible to take some steps which will advance or hold back the flowering date to some degree. Applying such procedures successfully, however, requires a good deal of experience with the particular plant or variety in question. It is very easy for an inexperienced grower to misjudge how long a plant will take to reach full flower based on the appearance of the swelling buds. There is often a considerable gap between the opening of the first one or two blooms and the flowering peak. Only growers able to maintain meticulous records are likely to apply these techniques with consistent success.

In order to bring forward the flowering time, the tree should be kept in a warm situation with full sun, and the watering should be strictly controlled. The aim is to supply just enough water to maintain the trees health and no more. This is a difficult procedure involving constant attention to the plant. If the tree is allowed to become too dry, the flowers will be ruined and harm may be done to the plant itself.

To hold back the flowering date, the Satsuki should be placed in a cool shady spot and the soil kept constantly damp.

Applying either of the above techniques for only a few weeks is only likely to alter the flowering dates by a few days. Any significant change in flowering date is likely to require a specific care regime applied consistently throughout the spring growing period.

End of the flowering period

For the Satsuki grower, it is the end of flowering which really marks the end of one annual cycle and the beginning of the next. The actions taken from this point on determine both the shape of the plant and its flowering performance for the following year.

Having completed flowering, the Satsuki is ready to embark on a period of strong vegetative growth. The plant is therefore able to recover strongly from major disturbance to its branch structure and root system. All the main work of pruning and repotting of established Satsuki bonsai should be done at this time.

The first task after the blossoms have withered is to remove all the dead flower heads from the plant. Developing seed capsules absorb a great deal of the plant's energy, so it is essential to remove the ovaries, not just the wilted petals. If this job is tackled as soon as the flowers wilt it is an easy matter to pull them off the plant by breaking the flower stems. If these stems are tough, this is a sign that the task should have been tackled sooner.

Removal of flower Heads

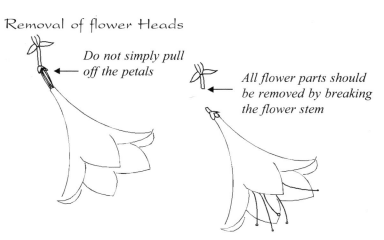

Do not simply pull off the petals

All flower parts should be removed by breaking the flower stem

Pruning

The annual pruning of an established Satsuki often follows a two- or three-year cycle. One year of hard reduction pruning, where twigs are thinned and shortened, is followed by a couple of years of lighter pruning. It is in these subsequent years that the best appearance and flowering performance is achieved.

Light Pruning

During the years of light pruning, new growth shoots are thinned to two at each terminal, and cut back to two leaves. Any twigs growing downwards or in towards the trunk are removed, as are any crossing branches. Any shoots showing an inclination to strong upward growth should also be cut back quite hard. This procedure is followed all over the tree, except that the apex is allowed a leaf or two more on each shoot, since it is the weakest part.

Providing that the bonsai has been correctly pruned in previous years, this may be all that is required, along with detail wiring of some wayward shoots. When treated in this manner, the foliage masses will become steadily larger and denser, and the pads will assume a more rounded profile. In order to maintain a clearly defined branch structure, and to halt this steady increase in foliage outline, it is necessary to alternate the light pruning regime with years when pruning is more severe.

Light pruning gives best flowering performance in the following year, but results in increased outlines and foliage density.

Thinning the current season's growth

At each branch terminal, remove all new shoots except two. Normally, shoots growing up or down are eliminated, leaving two horizontal shoots. Where growth is very strong, it may be appropriate to leave the two weakest shoots, while in weak areas of the plant, the two strongest are kept.

Unwanted shoots can be easily removed by bending them back in towards the trunk. They will break off cleanly where they emerge from last year's wood.

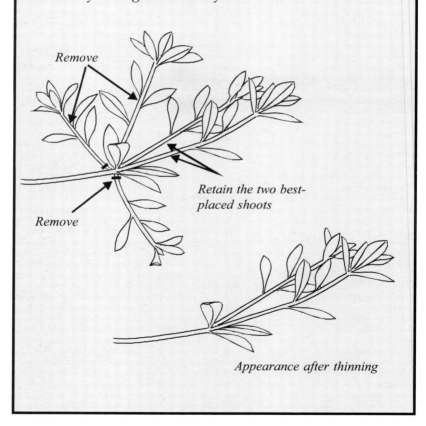

Remove

Retain the two best-placed shoots

Remove

Appearance after thinning

Trimming shoots to length

The severity of pruning varies from year to year and on different parts of the plant.

Below are typical pruning choices. Where a bonsai is to be exhibited in flower the following year, most shoots should be lightly trimmed back, leaving two leaves.

Where a reduction in foliage mass is required, various degrees of deeper pruning can be carried out, with differing results. In practice, all the different levels of pruning illustrated below are likely to be used on various parts of the same plant.

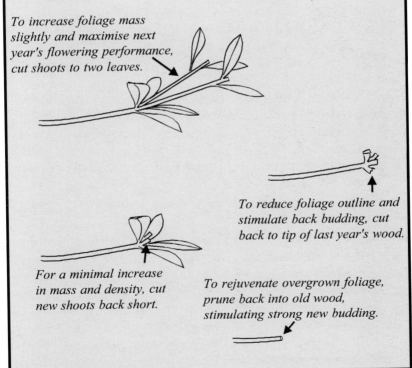

To increase foliage mass slightly and maximise next year's flowering performance, cut shoots to two leaves.

To reduce foliage outline and stimulate back budding, cut back to tip of last year's wood.

For a minimal increase in mass and density, cut new shoots back short.

To rejuvenate overgrown foliage, prune back into old wood, stimulating strong new budding.

Deep Pruning

The heavier pruning approach involves cutting back into the tree's old wood, shortening and thinning the branch- and twig-structure. A fairly thorough wiring of the branches is commonly done at the same time, in order to re-establish the design.

This heavier pruning approach might be necessary every second year if the Satsuki is of a vigorous variety, and if very well defined branch lines are important to the design. Other specimens which are less vigorous and/or have less demanding designs might need such treatment only once every three or four years.

A great advantage of Satsuki is that they will re-bud strongly, even on twigs and branches with no foliage. However, cutting back to old wood (recognised by its dark colour) is very stressful for the plant. Wherever possible (in terms of the design aims), one or two leaves, or even just a tiny stub of current year's shoot should be left. This ensures a much stronger and more rapid recovery. It is a risky procedure to apply total foliage removal to plants that have been neglected and are in a weak, very pot-bound condition. Such plants can be thinned, but leaves should be left on each twig that is retained. Only after they have fully regained their vigour should they be subjected to further reduction pruning.

Bonsai at the stage where they require deep pruning are usually covered in very dense foliage. This mass of foliage makes it very difficult to see where to prune because none of the twig structure is visible. The simplest first step is often to shear over the tops of the branch profiles as if trimming a hedge. This crude initial procedure clears away a good proportion of the leafy growth, making it much easier to see where one is cutting during the next stage.

The tasks of trimming and thinning then proceed in tandem. The aim is to produce a twig structure which is relatively flat in the horizontal plain. (The branch lines seen beneath the foliage should *NOT* be dead flat, however; there should be some gentle bends and undulations.) Seen from above, the branch should have a fan shape that steadily ramifies out towards the tips.

Thinning out the shoots follows normal bonsai principles. The aim is to have branches and twigs dividing into two at each junction. In practice, all growers must find what they consider an acceptable compromise between their ideal design and what the plant actually offers them. Where possible, branches which are considered too thick or badly

Branches should form a fan shape when viewed from above.

shaped should be eliminated, and younger, thinner branches used to fill the resulting gaps. Beginners often find it difficult to make these choices. Experience and the study of good models are the only real paths to skilful bonsai styling. The important point to recognize is that technical choices such as "which bits do you prune?" must always be made subject to a design framework.

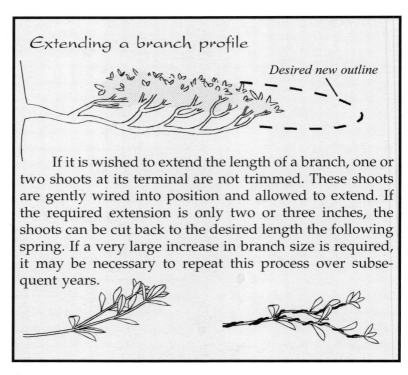

Extending a branch profile

Desired new outline

If it is wished to extend the length of a branch, one or two shoots at its terminal are not trimmed. These shoots are gently wired into position and allowed to extend. If the required extension is only two or three inches, the shoots can be cut back to the desired length the following spring. If a very large increase in branch size is required, it may be necessary to repeat this process over subsequent years.

Re-potting

When established Satsuki bonsai require re-potting, this is done immediately after flowering, at the same time as they are pruned and wired. They are vigorous plants with a dense, fine root system and require fairly frequent re-potting if they are to maintain their vigour. Frequency of re-potting varies, from every year for young, vigorous plants in smallish pots, to every two or three years for large old trees in big containers. Satsuki will survive without re-potting for much longer periods than this, but vigour steadily decreases and the disturbance of the roots, when it finally comes, is much more traumatic for the plant.

Re-potting

Roots should be gently combed out. Washing the soil away with a jet of water is helpful.

The root mass is trimmed back and evened out. Crossing roots, dead roots, etc. are removed. The area under the base of the trunk is pruned hard to prevent it becoming compacted.

Before placing in the pot, compost should be worked into any gaps in the bottom of the root-mass where air pockets might form. Spraying lightly with water will help to hold this soil in place.

The pot is prepared with a drainage course and tie wires. Soil should be worked carefully into all the gaps between the roots.

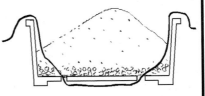

Satsuki differ significantly from other bonsai subjects with regard to roots and re-potting. With other types of bonsai, a priority is to preserve the very finest feeder roots. On a Satsuki, the very finest roots tend to die when disturbed by re-potting tools. Thus any fine roots exposed in re-potting should be trimmed back short. New feeder roots will quickly grow out from the larger roots to feed the plant. If a long "beard" of fine roots is left sticking out from the root-ball, this forms a layer of dead material between the plant and the new soil. New roots seem reluctant to penetrate this dead material, which can often be clearly seen as a dark line running through the soil when a tree grown in Kanuma is examined.

Satsuki send out feeder roots from all parts of the root system, not just from the extending tips of main roots. As a result, the central part of the root-ball becomes more and more densely packed, until it is impenetrable to air and water. One way to solve this problem is to cut wedges out of the root-ball, in towards the centre of the trunk. By gradually working around the plant at each re-potting, all of the root-ball is gradually renewed.

An alternative employed by Japanese growers is to give the tree an occasional "major" transplanting. Following several years of routine re-potting, the bonsai is removed from the pot and all the soil is washed off the roots using a powerful spray-jet. (This also removes all the feeder roots, fine dead material, etc.) This root-overhaul is combined with a major reduction-pruning of the tree, and the whole process has the effect of rejuvenating an old bonsai. If this major root overhaul was to be very severe, it might not be done after flowering as normal; instead, the process would be carried out in March or April, and all the flower buds would be removed from the tree. The bonsai would then be able to devote an entire season to recovery and vegetative growth.

Following re-potting, it is standard Japanese practice to cover the surface of the pot with a layer of sphagnum moss. This has the effect of maintaining the moisture levels and allowing a less frequent watering regime while the root system is recovering. Otherwise, Satsuki are given standard bonsai aftercare: the tree is placed in a lightly shaded spot and given regular foliage misting; great care is taken not to over-water, and fertilizer is given only when clear signs of new growth are seen.

Care after mid-summer

Satsuki form their flower buds for the following year in mid- to late-summer. It is important to be aware that any pruning at this time can have a serious effect on flower production. In general it is best to avoid any pruning after mid-July, other than to remove unwanted buds, sprouts, downward growth etc.. If necessary, other untidy growths can be trimmed in early autumn, once the flower buds can be seen.

Training-wire should be watched very carefully and removed as soon as it shows signs of biting in. This can happen in as little as four weeks in some cases. Removal of wire can be a very awkward task on a Satsuki, as dense foliage can make it difficult to see. Cutting wires off is strongly recommended and is almost essential with heavier gauges.

A good collection of Satsuki showing autumn colour is a spectacular sight. It is well worth the effort to clean up and tidy bonsai in order to enjoy them at this time of year. Different varieties show different colours, with yellows, or-anges and rich wine-reds making superb contrasts with the deep green summer leaves.

Winter care

Ideally, Satsuki should be exposed to steadily decreasing temperatures during the early part of the winter, then moved into a cold greenhouse, or similar, when prolonged spells of severe cold become likely. Growers should be prepared to supply protection earlier, should a severe cold snap be forecast. Protecting Satsuki before severe weather arrives is generally a bad thing. Winter hardiness is greatly increased if the plants are able to become gradually accustomed to colder weather.

Another reason for avoiding early winter protection concerns the setting of flower buds. Although flower buds are formed in late summer, these buds will often fail to develop into flowers unless they have been cold set. This entails the plant being subject to temperatures below about 10 degrees centigrade for four to eight weeks. If plants fail to develop flowers, despite the appearance of buds the previous summer, it may be because they were placed into winter quarters too early, and that these quarters were too warm.

Plants should be given a final spray of insecticide before being placed in winter quarters. Routine spraying with fungicide should continue through the winter. All dead leaves and other debris should be cleared from the plant and the soil surface, and maximum available ventilation should be provided at every opportunity. This is most important. Fungal infections can be a severe problem if plants are packed in poorly ventilated greenhouses over winter.

Ventilation of greenhouses is also very important in the early spring, because unseasonably warm weather can start Satsuki into growth too early. This renders the new growth susceptible to a hard, late frost.

Chapter Eight

From
Raw Material
To
Bonsai

Production of a Satsuki bonsai from raw material

Sources of material for Satsuki bonsai are similar to those for other bonsai subjects:

a) A large field-grown plant can be cut down, and the stump used as the basis of a heavy-trunked bonsai.

b) A propagation can be grown-on until big enough to start bonsai training.

c) A part-trained, imported commercial bonsai can be purchased.

Unfortunately, option a) is not really applicable to western growers, because there are no available field-grown Satsuki to dig up.

Option b) is relatively cheap and straightforward, providing that a parent plant is available or, alternatively, a source where young plants may be purchased. Propagation of Satsuki is not particularly difficult and plants can be produced by means of cuttings or air-layerings. Satsuki also grow readily from seed, but in this case the quality of flowers obtained is very variable.

The disadvantage of starting from a piece of young material is obviously the time it takes to produce a bonsai of any substantial size. This is an important consideration if the grower considers a big impressive trunk to be one of main attractions of Satsuki.

The final option, of buying an imported tree, has the advantage of supplying a substantial piece of material to work with immediately. The down-side of this approach being the considerable cost involved. Satsuki are expensive in Japan and this is reflected in the prices of imported trees.

As with too many Satsuki imported into Europe, this one did not have an accurate variety name. It is probably **Gyoten**.

*A Satsuki of the variety **Hinotsukasa** in full bloom.*

In the case of large trees with good quality trunks, there is also a very limited supply.

A purchased import will generally require a lot of work before it can be considered a fine bonsai, but results do not take long to achieve if care is taken to purchase a suitable trunk. This is the key to buying a good bonsai of any kind. Providing that the trunk is of good quality, all the branches, twigs, etc. can be developed in a relatively short time. A poor trunk, however, never gets any better.

The worst-case scenario when purchasing a Satsuki, is for the buyer to be seduced into buying a clump of gorgeous flowers, only to discover a week or two later that these flowers were disguising an extremely ugly bonsai. A golden rule is to remember that the tree is without flowers for more than ninety per cent of the time and to choose accordingly.

Training trees from cuttings

The details of propagation are well covered in other texts. This section aims to cover the development of a plant from a rooted cutting to a bonsai.

Finished bonsai require adult flowering growth, but when a young Satsuki is being grown on, it is juvenile, "sprout" type growth that needs to be encouraged.

If left to its own devices, a typical Satsuki plant of three or four years old would have half a dozen or more trunks emerging from the ground. The height of such a plant is unlikely to be more than a foot and, in the case of dwarf varieties, might be only a few inches.

The height reached and the growth habit displayed by a young plant is to some extent determined by the type of parent material from which the cutting was taken. If the cutting has been taken from a flowering branch, then the new plant will produce very compact growth and will probably flower in the year following rooting. If the cutting has come from a sprout, the plant will grow much faster and will take longer to flower. These two points are directly related. Whenever a Satsuki shoot develops flower buds, it ceases any attempt to increase in height. The multiple-trunk form of young Satsuki results from the fact that strong growth of each shoot stops as it forms flower buds, and the

Initial development of a cutting

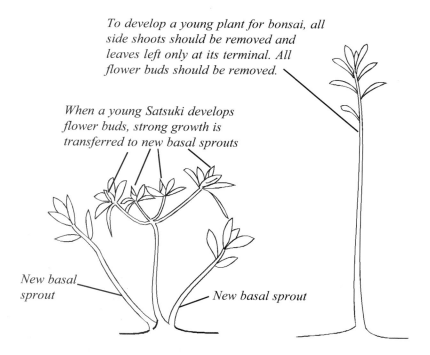

To develop a young plant for bonsai, all side shoots should be removed and leaves left only at its terminal. All flower buds should be removed.

When a young Satsuki develops flower buds, strong growth is transferred to new basal sprouts

New basal sprout

New basal sprout

growth energy is redirected to the production of new sprouts from the base of the plant. The plant therefore develops it natural form as a wide, low, ground-hugging bush.

Removal of Flower Buds

If a young plant is producing flower buds which are interfering with growth, it is desirable to remove these. The buds can be removed in the autumn as soon as they are large enough to handle. Varieties which produce large flower buds before winter can be bud-stripped several weeks before those bearing small buds. This is a delicate and time-consuming operation which is best carried out using tweezers, particularly for small buds. The new growth buds sprout from immediately below the flower bud and great care must be taken not to damage these new growth points. It will be found that buds on some varieties break away easily, while others are difficult. Where buds resist breaking off, it is very easy to damage the plant itself.

Initial Trunk Shaping

The initial wire shaping of the trunk can be carried out after two to four years of growth, depending on the size of the plant and how big a final bonsai is planned. If a very small bonsai is planned then shaping should be done as soon as possible. For large bonsai it is best to let the plant make a good height first. Earlier shaping is easier because the young trunk is more flexible. Japanese commercial practice is to apply this trunk wire in the autumn, but remember that frost protection is essential for wired trees. An advantage of wiring at this time is that the plants have lower sap levels and consequently are not quite so brittle. They are also less susceptible to having the bark scraped off. Initial wiring can also be done in spring or early summer, but great care must be taken to observe the plants for signs of the wire biting in because this happens extremely quickly on young plants during the main growing season.

The wire for bending the trunk should be pushed firmly into the soil, taking care not to damage any potential surface roots. (Judicious scraping away of the soil is recommended before inserting the wire.) As when wiring any bonsai, the stiffness of the wire must match the stiffness of the branch being bent. Given the brittle nature of Satsuki and their delicate bark, it is often easier and safer to apply two thinner wires rather than one thick one.

After applying the wire, it is best to picture the desired trunk shape before commencing any bending. Once the trunk has thickened it will be impossible to change the shape, so this one task may be the most important in establishing the future quality of the plant as a bonsai.

Deciding how many bends to put in the trunk and how severe these should be, is quite difficult. The grower needs a clear idea of the final dimensions the plant will have as a bonsai, and what sort of trunk diameter it will be grown on to before beginning bonsai training. Competence in bonsai styling cannot be learned by reading books. The best route to attaining the skills is through practice combined with the careful study of as many good bonsai as possible.

Many Satsuki imported from Japan are poor quality examples of the Repeated "S" style. These often have grotesquely exaggerated and artificial-looking curves. This type of extreme bending is to be avoided at all costs. On the other hand, it is important to remember that bends will become much less severe as the trunk thickens. When trunks are grown on to very large dimensions, curves that once looked highly exaggerated can almost disappear.

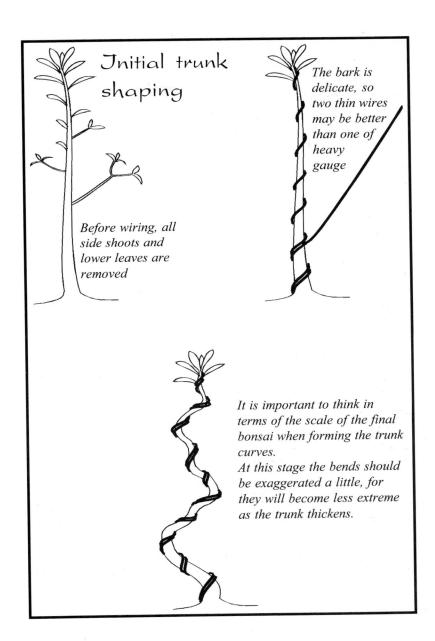

Initial trunk shaping

Before wiring, all side shoots and lower leaves are removed

The bark is delicate, so two thin wires may be better than one of heavy gauge

It is important to think in terms of the scale of the final bonsai when forming the trunk curves.
At this stage the bends should be exaggerated a little, for they will become less extreme as the trunk thickens.

Trunk development

In order to train a young Satsuki into a bonsai, the first task is to fatten the trunk. The scale of the required end result determines the time taken for this stage of the tree's development. A grower of shohin Satsuki might begin branch training after only a year or two; on the other hand it takes decades in a growing bed to produce the large Informal Upright trunks which are so popular in Japan today.

The young trunk is planted out in a growing bed and allowed to grow unchecked for a couple of years. The plant is then severely pruned, which stimulates an explosion of vigorous sprout activity from all parts of the trunk. This cycle is repeated until the desired trunk dimensions are achieved.

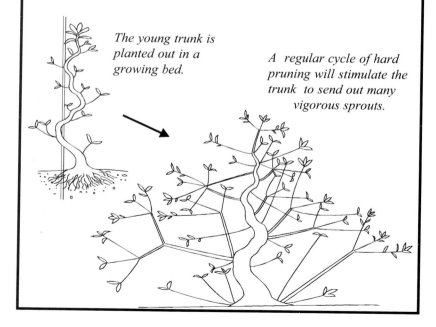

The young trunk is planted out in a growing bed.

A regular cycle of hard pruning will stimulate the trunk to send out many vigorous sprouts.

Branch training

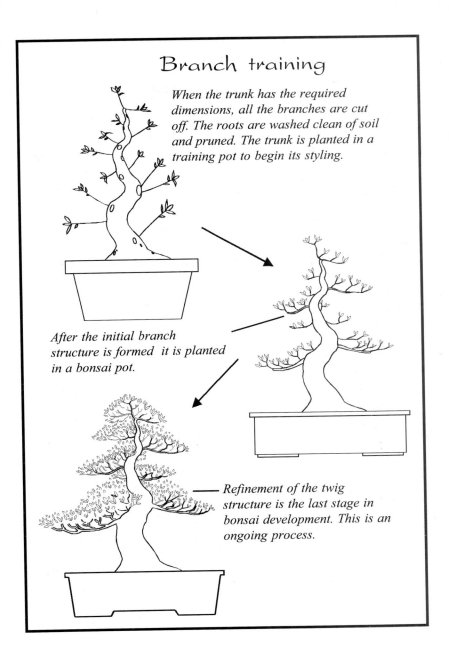

When the trunk has the required dimensions, all the branches are cut off. The roots are washed clean of soil and pruned. The trunk is planted in a training pot to begin its styling.

After the initial branch structure is formed it is planted in a bonsai pot.

Refinement of the twig structure is the last stage in bonsai development. This is an ongoing process.

The other thing to avoid when shaping trunks, is the perfect text-book Informal Upright shape. This appears as a diagram in many bonsai books, but it should be seen as an illustration of basic styling principles, not something to be copied exactly. - Real trees are much more unpredictable and eccentric.

Trunk development

Wire should be left on the trunk until it is just starting to bite. The young tree will then be set in its new shape and the programme of trunk-fattening can begin. In Japan, commercial quality trees are thickened in fields or nursery beds, while high quality trees are often thickened using deep beds inside poly-tunnels. The best approach for a British grower would probably be to plant the young tree in a large pot or growing box, unless it is possible to construct a suitable bed in a greenhouse.

When planting out the young trunk, the root system should be evened out, and any high roots, or roots which cross over others, should be removed. This will give the plant a good start towards an attractive root system. After this root-pruning, the tall leggy trunk may need staking until it becomes established. From this point on, the aim is to take advantage of the Satsuki habit of sending out strong sprout growth as a response to pruning. Every two years or so, all the branches should be pruned back very hard and this stimulates new sprouts from all over the trunk. Sprouts growing at or below soil level should be removed frequently. The only regular requirements for the plant during this process are water and fertilizer plus an occasional pesticide spray.

The move to a training pot

The time will come when the Satsuki trunk has reached a suitable size to begin its bonsai training. There is no correct point at which training should begin, it is often the impatience of the grower which determines how long the tree is allowed to fatten. The tree is then lifted from the growing bed and begins its life in a container. This is the stage at which most Japanese enthusiasts like to buy their trees. Japanese Satsuki magazines are crammed with advertisements showing photographs of untrained trunks for sale at the just-lifted-from-the-ground stage. Unfortunately, plants at this interesting stage are not available for sale in the West, because trees exported from Japan have always had some initial branch training.

The trunk should be lifted from the bed with a generous root-ball. Take care to ensure that the roots do not dry out while you carry out work on the top of the plant.

The work on the trunk consists of cutting it down to the required height and removing any significant branches which will not be part of the final design. If there are any small shoots which have potential for development as branches, these are left on with a minimal amount of foliage. A few other small shoots may be left at the apex, or around major wounds. The foliage on these small growths will help to sustain sap flow while the trunk re-buds.

As stated in an earlier chapter, there is a danger of sap withdrawal if large branches are suddenly removed from any but the most vigorous plants. If in doubt, it is safer to remove the branch in stages. All wounds on the trunk must be carefully sealed.

The next stage is to prepare the roots for potting. A strong jet of water should be used to remove all the soil from the roots. The roots themselves are then cut back to the size and shape of the pot. This first training pot will probably have to be considerably larger than the final choice of container, but Satsuki have well-branched root systems which can be reduced very hard. Particular care should be taken to even out the top of the root system. All crossing roots should be removed, or straightened and pegged in place. The aim is to accentuate the natural Satsuki trunk flare by leaving only those surface roots which slope downwards and outwards at a suitable angle. Any twisted or eccentric knuckle-roots which break this line down into the soil should be removed, unless, of course, they are large enough and interesting enough to really form a primary feature of the bonsai design.

Potting up the new bonsai follows standard practice, but these newly potted trees should always be tied or wired into the container. This keeps them stable until new fine feeder roots can form. The soil mix used should be very porous. Whether Kanuma, or a humus-based compost is used, it should be sieved and the fines discarded. Adding chopped sphagnum moss to Kanuma is very important when severe root pruning is carried out as it helps the production of new roots. A thick layer of sphagnum (or even coarse peat, if sphagnum is not available) should be placed over the soil surface to maintain the humidity. This layer of moss should be removed when new white roots are seen starting to grow up into it.

The move from growing bed to pot is commonly undertaken in spring. The tree is then allowed a recovery period and fed to encourage a crop of strong new shoots.

Initial branch selection

The shoots which will be used to form the basic branch structure of the new bonsai should not be chosen until the plant has an abundant head of healthy new growth. This may take only a few months in some cases, while others may require a full year of recovery. All the new shoots which will not form part of the final design are then eliminated and those selected for branches are wired into position. This is another of the crucial stages in a bonsai's development. The angle at which the branches spring from the trunk is determined now, and this is one of the main determinants of the tree's style. Once the branches have grown and set into position, this basic branch angle can be altered only by removing all these branches and starting again.

The wire on the new branches must be checked very regularly and removed in good time. The young branches should be allowed to lengthen without a check, unless one particular part of the plant, usually the apex, is showing much less vigour than the rest. In that case the strongest growths should be cut back to allow the weaker parts to catch up a little.

The whole process of selection, thinning out and wiring should be repeated the following spring, and it will often be possible to select and wire again by mid-summer. In this way the new branch-pads are quickly built up. By the end of the second year the tree should be starting to look like a genuine bonsai, though the foliage pads will probably still be much too small in proportion to the trunk.

Choice of pot

At this point consideration can be given to what sort of bonsai container will be appropriate for the finished tree.

Some bonsai seem immediately to suggest an appropriate size and form of pot, while for other designs an acceptable choice is arrived at only after a long struggle. Where a suitable pot design does not come to mind, the best idea is to examine photographs of similar trees for inspiration. If that fails to suggest a solution, take the tree along to a stockist of bonsai containers, and try a selection of styles and sizes against it.

While less common containers such as drum pots, primitives, or ceramic slabs may be just right for particular trees, the majority of Satsuki seem to look best in either oval pots or soft-cornered rectangles. Containers chosen for Satsuki often seem quite deep by normal bonsai standards. If a plain pot looks too heavy, due to this extra depth, one with a rim and horizontal beading will appear less deep and therefore lighter.

The reason for selecting deeper pots for Satsuki is that they allow an even soil-moisture content to be maintained much more easily. It is possible to use shallow containers, but watering is needed several times a day in hot weather and some shading from the Sun may be required to prevent heat stress.

Appendices, Glossary and Further Reading

Appendix One - Satsuki flower patterns

Arare-shibori (Hail variegation) - The flower is densely covered in fairly large specks and streaks of colour.

Date-shibori (Showy variegation) - The white background is covered in many strong stripes of various widths.

Fukurin (Jewel border) - The dark coloured flower is edged with a white border. This border varies from wide to very narrow depending on the variety and the junction of white and colour is often irregular. Sometimes referred to as Shirofukurin (white jewel border).

Hakeme-shibori (Brushed variegation) - The flower is covered in many long parallel lines.

Hanzome (Half-coloured) - The flower is divided into two major colour segments.

Harusame (Spring rain) - The entire flower is covered with a fairly even pattern of fine flecks and spots.

Saizaki - This refers to a flower form where the petals are very long and narrow, and are separate to the base.

Sokojiro (White throat) - A coloured flower with a white centre.

Tamafu (Jewel spot) - Each petal fades to a pale centre.

Tobiiri-shibori (Patchy variegation) - A white flower with a few scattered splashes of colour.

Appendix Two - Satsuki varieties mentioned in this book

Dai-seiko (Great starlight) - White with occasional stripes of deep pink, varying to deep pink selfs with a narrow white *fukurin* border. The wide-spaced, pointed petals are turned back at the ends. (2"-2.5").

Eikan (A garland) - Flowers are large (3"-4") with a ruffled edge; most are white with a green blotch. Occasional flowers are part pink, rarely all pink. Pink flowers have a deeper pink blotch.

Hi-gasa (Parasol) - Very large flowers with wide, wavy petals (4"-5"). Colour is a rich purplish-pink with a rose blotch.

Hiodoshi (Scarlet-threaded suit of armour) - Very good sokojiro form. Flowers are a strong red with the centre being white to faint pink. Slightly bell-shaped flowers with round-ended spaced lobes. (2"-2.5").

Kinsai (Golden tassel) - The classic saizaki variety; described by Ito in the 1690's under the name Zai. Flowers are deep reddish-orange with petals being long and contorted. Stamens are very long and prominent.

Kozan (Brilliant mountain) - Very neat flowers with spaced, rounded petals; very pale pink to off white (1.5"). Variable and very prone to sporting different colours, flower forms, petal numbers, etc.. Very slow bushy growth.

Shin-kyo (Divine mirror) - The type flower is of tamafu pattern, with pale centres and deeper pink edges. Many deeper pink selfs are produced, along with occasional white blooms. Petals are rounded and slightly spaced.

Shira-fuji (White Mount Fuji) - This variety is most noted for its variegated foliage; green bordered creamy-white. The flowers are white with some speckles and stripes of purplish pink. Occasional purple selfs. The flower form is somewhat irregular, but blooming is profuse and very long lasting. (1.5"-2").

Shiraito-no-taki (White thread waterfall) - Extreme saizaki type. White with the odd purplish strip. Flowers are very irregular with some or all of the petals missing on most blooms and the white stamens very distinct.

Shuku-fuku (Celebration) - Large pink flowers with many variations and markings in other pinks. Wide, round petals (3"-4").

Tama-no-hada (Pearl complexion) - Very large flowers with wide round petals (4"-5"). White with deep pink stripes, and strong to deep pink selfs.

Yata-no-kagami (Sacred mirror) - Tamafu type. Blush pink centres shading to deep coral around the edges. Some flowers are much deeper coloured but with the same tamafu pattern; others are coral selfs with a dark blotch. Spaced petals (2"-2.5").

Glossary

0-10-10 Fertilizer

A zero-nitrogen fertilizer, often used by bonsai growers in autumn. This feed strengthens the tree without inducing fresh growth.

Air-layering

A propagation technique where a ring of bark is removed from a suitable branch or trunk. The area is then dusted with hormone rooting-powder and wrapped with moist sphagnum moss. The plant responds to the wounding process by issuing new roots immediately above the wound site. When enough roots have grown to support the new propagation it is separated from the parent plant.

Akadama

Japanese red-clay potting soil widely used for bonsai. It has an excellent granular structure which drains well and promotes good root growth. Unlike most clay soils, Akadama has a relatively low nutrient-holding capacity and is best suited to a continuous, low-level feeding regime. Akadama eventually breaks down to fine particles and it must be replaced before this stage is reached.

Apical dominance

Most plants depend on rapid upward growth in order to compete for space and light. They achieve this by concentrating their growth energies at the apex, or growing point, of their upper shoots. Satsuki are, by contrast, basally dominant; in other words they concentrate their energies on the outward spread of their lowest shoots.

Biogold

A Japanese-made organic fertilizer. Pellets are placed on the soil surface and a small quantity of nutrient is washed into the soil at each watering. This gives the constant but very gentle feeding which is ideal for bonsai. Biogold has given particularly good results when used on Satsuki bonsai.

Branch sports

This refers to genetic mutations occurring within an individual plant, so that certain branches exhibit different characteristics from the rest. If a Satsuki branch sport can be reliably propagated by vegetative means, it may be given a new variety name of its own.

Calcined clay

Graded clay granules which are fired in a kiln to a temperature where they just change into ceramic. These are resistant to physical breakdown; they drain very freely indeed, and, being absorbent, they hold a good reservoir of water. Bonsai composts using calcined clay are generally superior to those using only grit as a filler. Biosorb is the most popular calcined clay used for bonsai in Britain.

Chelated Trace elements

Nutrient elements required by plants in very small amounts. Micronutrients are generally supplied in chelated form, which means they are specially prepared to be easily taken up by the plant roots. In addition to the major nutrients (Nitrogen, Phosphorous and Potassium), azaleas need small quantities of Iron, Magnesium, Manganese, Boron and **Calcium**. Azaleas are generally stated to be haters of Calcium, but this is not really true. The problem is that azaleas have evolved on soils which are very deficient in Calcium. The plants have therefore adapted by becoming super-efficient at absorbing any Calcium available. Unfortunately, when an azalea is planted in a limey soil with a lot of free Calcium, it is unable to switch off this absorbtion capability, and continues to take Calcium up in preference to other needed elements.

Satsuki require trace elements in very small quantities indeed and it is very easy to create a fresh set of problems through overdose.

Cut-paste

A Japanese compound for sealing tree wounds. This material has the consistency of Plasticine and remains flexible in use. It promotes rapid healing of large wounds and the new callous growth is able to spread under the paste.

Enmag

A specialised fertilizer compound for Rhododendrons and azaleas.

Evergreen garden azaleas

The evergreen, spring-flowering azaleas commonly grown in British gardens. Also called Japanese azaleas. In Japan these azaleas are called *Tsutsuji*.

Ito Ihei

A gardener and nurseryman of the early Edo era. His monograph on azaleas, the Kinshi Makura (1692), was almost certainly the world's first book devoted to a single group of plants.

Insulating fleece

A lightweight blanket of unwoven synthetic material, which can be laid directly onto plants and provides several degrees of frost protection. Because it allows light to penetrate, this material can be left in place for some time, though care must be taken to ensure adequate ventilation.

Kanuma

A yellowish, acid sub-soil dug in the region of Kanuma city in Japan. This soil has a low nutrient capacity, good drainage and very extensive pore space, all of which make it an ideal growing medium for mature Satsuki. It is obtainable from good bonsai nurseries.

Kinshi Makura (A Brocade Pillow)

Book by Ito Ihei on the subject of azaleas. This was the first work to systematically divide azaleas into *Tsutsuji* and Satsuki.

Kiyonal

A Japanese wound-sealant, used for relatively small cuts, or where very rapid callousing is not essential.

Meika

Satsuki trained and exhibited for the appreciation of the flowers only. Normally grown in the Repeated "S" style.

Mie Satsuki

Also called "hedge Satsuki". These are a distinct group of Satsuki bred for growing as clipped bushes in Japanese gardens. Named after Mie prefecture in Japan where many are produced.

Miracid

A widely-available soluble fertilizer and soil-acidifier; used for all ericaceous plants, and recommended for Satsuki.

Mutations

Changes in the genetic material of an organism, which can lead to changes in the observed physical characteristics. Mutations can be induced by external agents such as radiation or certain chemicals. In the case of Satsuki, some of the genetic material may be inherently unstable.

pH range

A system used in horticulture to measure the concentration of Hydrogen ions in the soil water. This gives a measurement of the acidity or alkalinity of the soil. A pH of 7 is neutral. Figures below 7 are acid and above it are alkaline. It is a logarithmic scale with pH 5 being ten times more acid than pH6, and pH4 being ten times more acid than pH5, etc.

Sequestrene

One of the earliest chelated Iron supplementary feeds to be developed. Modern Sequestrene compounds include other essential trace elements.

Shibori

Variegated markings on a flower. It literally means "tie-dyed". Some Japanese experts distinguish between dozens of different *shibori* patterns on Satsuki flowers.

Shohin

Very small, easily portable bonsai. The Japanese do not tend to define such terms by precise measurements. Whether a bonsai is classed as a shohin is judged more by its character than its dimensions. (Literally means "small goods".)

Soil acidifiers

Chemicals added to the soil or water in order to increase the soil acidity. For garden soil the most common acidifier is Sulphur. For Satsuki bonsai, Miracid is often used for its acidifying properties.

Sports

Genetically altered plants with characteristics which distinguish them from the parent variety or type.

Tsutsuji

Spring-flowering evergreen azaleas.

Varietal drift

The tendency for a variety to change over long periods of time or, more particularly, the tendency for an isolated group of plants to move away from the original varietal type. This is a particular problem when genetically unstable plants such as Satsuki are propagated by vegetative means.

Winter hardiness

The ability of plants to withstand a given severity of winter weather. This is not in reality a single objective measure, but a complex interaction of many factors.

Further Reading

Japanese language

Sources of information on Satsuki are abundant in Japanese language. Some of these Japanese publications can be of great value to western enthusiasts simply for their splendid colour photographs.

The publications listed below are a few which are likely to be of particular value to the non-Japanese reader:-

Satsuki Kenkyusha (Satsuki Research magazine)

This is a beautiful monthly colour magazine devoted entirely to Satsuki.

Tochinoha Shobo Dictionary of Satsuki Varieties

This is the bible for Satsuki enthusiasts. Over 900 varieties of Satsuki are illustrated in full colour. Though the text is in Japanese, the name of each variety is also printed in Romaji (latinised text), which is the way we refer to them in the West.

Japan Satsuki Association – National Exhibition Albums

Beautiful hardback books of photographs. Produced annually, these albums are packed with inspiring full colour pictures of the exhibits at the Japanese National Satsuki Exhibition, which is held in Ueno Park, Tokyo, at the beginning of June each year.

(The above publications are sold by Alexander Kennedy.)

Publications in English

General texts on azaleas

Azaleas; by Fred C. Galle; Timber Press, 1987

This huge book is the standard monograph on azalea species and their hybrids. A chapter on Satsuki is included, with a long descriptive list of many varieties available in the U.S.A.

The Azalea Book; by Frederic P. Lee; Theophrastus

A much older book than the one above (first published 1958). Though somewhat superseded by Galle's monograph, it still contains a lot of good general information on azalea culture.

Rhododendrons and Azaleas; by Judith Beresford; Faber & Faber, 1973

This is an old book, (first published in 1964) but it can still be found in libraries. It gives some very good information on the culture of rhododendrons and azaleas. In particular, it gives one of the clearest explanations to be found of trace element deficiencies and how they relate to an excess of free calcium in the soil.

The book's greatest interest is perhaps as a historical document illustrating a traditional English view of the subject. Reading it does much to explain why there is so little awareness of Satsuki among British gardeners, for while it is a very learned text, with profuse use of Latin, there is nowhere an acknowledgement, or even, apparently, an awareness that the world's greatest experts on evergreen azaleas reside in Japan. Satsuki receive what amounts to a small footnote on the final page.

Historical background

A Brocade Pillow - Azaleas of Old Japan; by Ito Ihei; (translation by Kaname Kato; commentary by John L. Creech); Weatherhill

This book is a translation of the classic "Kinshi Makura", first published in 1692. It is an essential reference for anyone interested in the history of Japanese azaleas. The original woodblock illustrations are reproduced and the modern commentary helps clarify some of Ito's obscure and occasionally eccentric descriptions.

Information on Satsuki Bonsai

Bonsai Techniques For Satsuki; by John Y. Naka, Richard K. Ota and Kenko Rokkaku; Ota Bonsai Nursery, 1979

This classic book is the only previous major publication on Satsuki in English. It is now in short supply and quite hard to find. Unfortunately, specific information on Satsuki culture takes up only a small part of the book. The remainder is really a beginner's guide to Bonsai, using Satsuki as models.

Satsuki Azaleas as Dwarfed Potted Shrubs; by Tomisaku Ugajin; Article published in the Brooklin Botanic Garden Handbook on Dwarfed Potted Trees, 1953

The Brooklin Handbook was a landmark publication

representing the first serious attempt to inform English-speaking readers about bonsai in Japan. The article on Satsuki is interesting both as a historical document and for the photographs, which give a good indication of how Japanese tastes have changed in forty years..

Other sources on Satsuki Bonsai include articles in the following periodicals:-

Bonsai Today

Bonsai Magazine (U.K.)

Bonsai Clubs International

International Bonsai

General books on bonsai

This book has been written with the assumption that the reader would have at least an elementary knowledge of bonsai. Should you wish to learn more about bonsai in general, the following are good introductory books:-

The Complete Book of Bonsai; by Harry Tomlinson

The Bonsai Book; by Dan Barton; Ebury Press, 1989

Bonsai - The Art of Growing and Keeping Miniature Trees; by Peter Chan; Apple Press, 1985

Index

Index

soil acidifier 48
sokojiro 30, 36, 40, 41, 74
sphagnum moss 47, 91, 106
sporting behaviour 39
sports 34, 39
"sprout" type growth 65
striped flowers 42
styling 21
surface roots 100
systemic fungicide 51

T

Tama-no-hada 28
Tamafu 32
tamafu 74
the name Satsuki 13
the Satsuki growth cycle 62
thinning new growth 84
throat blotch 30
tie-dye pattern. *See* "shibori"
Tobiiri-shibori 31
trace elements 49
training pot 105
trunk flare 106
trunks 20
Tsutsuji 12
twig structure 87

V

variegated leaves. 14
varietal drift 43
vine weevil 49

W

water 47
water requirements 74

white throat. *See* sokojiro
winter care 92
winter hardiness 34
winter protection 52
wiring Satsuki 68

Y

Yata-no-kagami 32

Alexander Kennedy

Bonsai Nurseryman

Specialist in Satsuki Azaleas
Maker of Fine Bonsai Containers

Satsuki

from rooted cuttings to fine specimen bonsai

Also
Accessories and tools
Kanuma soil
Satsuki publications

Please write or telephone for our mail-order price list

Splatt Pottery, Tresmeer, Launceston,
Cornwall PL15 8QX England

Telephone (01566)781440